NEW JERSEY
BEACH
DIVER
By Daniel &
Denise Berg

THE DIVER'S GUIDE TO
NEW JERSEY BEACH DIVING SITES
Contributing Writers, Bill Davis and Howard Rothweiler

DISCLAIMER

Please be aware that the information contained in this book is only a supplement to proper diving instruction. Reading this book does not qualify a diver to do dives or to participate in any activity beyond the capabilities of his own qualifications experience and training.

Please use the information contained within this book as a basic guideline. Let good diving skills, common sense, and courtesy lead you and your dive buddy to safely enjoy exploring New Jersey's coast.

Library of Congress Catalog Card No. 92-074469
ISBN: 0-9616167-8-4

FOR ADDITIONAL COPIES, WRITE TO:
AQUA EXPLORERS, INC.
P.O. Box 116
East Rockaway, N.Y. 11518
Phone/Fax (516) 868-2658
Toll Free (800) 695-7585

ABOUT THE AUTHORS

Photo by Rick Schwarz.

Dan Berg is a P.A.D.I. (Professional Association of Diving Instructors) Master Scuba Diver Trainer. He is a Specialty Instructor in Wreck Diving, Night Diving, Search and Recovery, Underwater Hunting, Deep Diving, Dry Suit Diving, U/W Metal Detector Hunting, U/W Archeology, and has written and teaches his own nationally approved Distinctive Specialties in Shipwreck Research, Shipwreck Sketching and U/W Cinematography. Dan also holds certifications in Rescue, U/W photography, Medic First Aid, Oxygen Administration and Environmental Marine Ecology and is a member of the American Sport Divers Association and Eastern Dive Boat Association. Dan is the author of the original WRECK VALLEY book, a record of shipwrecks off Long Island's South Shore, SHORE DIVER, a diver's guide to Long Island's beach sites, WRECK VALLEY Vol II, a record of shipwrecks off Long Island's South shore and New Jersey, co-author of TROPICAL SHIPWRECKS, a vacationing diver's guide to the Bahamas and Caribbean, and BERMUDA SHIPWRECKS, a vacationing diver's guide to Bermuda's shipwrecks, SHIPWRECK DIVING, a complete diver's handbook to mastering the skills of wreck diving, FLORIDA SHIPWRECKS, the diver's guide to shipwrecks around the state of Florida and the Florida keys, publisher of the Wreck Valley LORAN C COORDINATE LIST, executive producer and host of the DIVE WRECK VALLEY CABLE Television and video series, and SHIPWRECKS OF GRAND CAYMAN VIDEO. His award winning underwater cinematography has been used on a variety of cable TV shows, including LONG ISLAND ALL OUTDOORS, LONG ISLAND FISHING, FOX 5 NEWS, CBS NEWS, EYE WITNESS NEWS, NEWS 12 and DIVER'S DOWN. Dan's photographs and shipwreck articles have been published in SKIN DIVER MAGAZINE, UNDERWATER USA, NAUTICAL BRASS, The FISHERMAN, FISHEYE VIEW, SHIPWRECKS, NAUTILUS, EASTERN & WESTERN TREASURES, THE SUB AQUA JOURNAL, SHIPS AND SHIPWRECKS, TREASURE MAGAZINE, NEW YORK OUTDOORS plus many more.

Denise Berg is a P.A.D.I. certified open water diver with specialty ratings in Underwater Photography, Equipment Maintenance, Shipwreck Research and is also a certified Regulator Repair Technician. Denise is co-author of the books TROPICAL SHIPWRECKS, BERMUDA SHIPWRECKS and FLORIDA SHIPWRECKS and has done underwater modeling. Denise has had her articles published in SKIN DIVER MAGAZINE, SHIPWRECKS, NAUTICAL BRASS, DISCOVER DIVING, THE SUB AQUA JOURNAL and SHIPS AND SHIPWRECKS, and she is a script writer for the DIVE WRECK VALLEY cable television series.

ACKNOWLEDGEMENTS

We would like to thank the following for their time, knowledge, information and participation in this project. Christine Berg for editing and proof reading; George Baluski at Dover One Hour Photo, Captain Steve Bielenda, Captain Kevin Brennan, Cathie Cush, Bill Davis, George Dreher, Patricia W. Geffken, Richard M. Geffken, Gary Gentile, Andre Hutchinson, Dave Keller, Jozef Koppelman, Dan Lieb, Frank Litter, Dr. Steve Lombardo, Ed Maliszewski, Carlos Narciso, Mark Promislow, Howard Rothweiler, Bill Schmoldt, Rick Schwarz, Dave Schwartzman, Herb Segars, Al Vogel; last, but certainly not least, Winfred M. Berg, and Donald Berg for their continued support and technical advice.

CONTRIBUTING WRITERS

When we started to research the shipwrecks off New Jersey's coast and the different beach diving sites that divers were enjoying we came accross two individuals who were not only extremely knowledgeable and experienced beach divers but who had already accumulated a wealth of beach diving information. Bill Davis and Howard Rothweiler had been working on their own beach diving book. Fortunately, Bill and Howard decided to join us and together we have compiled all of our information into one NEW JERSEY BEACH DIVER book. Much of the information contained within this text is due to the efforts, experience and research of Bill Davis and Howard Rothweiler.

UNDERWATER PHOTOGRAPHY

We would like to acknowledge and sincerely thank the following for their beautiful underwater photographs. A picture is worth a thousand words, and the photos taken by these professionals capture all the beauty, mystery, thrill and excitement of diving off New Jersey's beaches. We are grateful to Captain Kevin Brennan, Cathie Cush, Jozef Koppelman, Herb Segars, and Rick Schwarz.

HOW TO USE

All the beach sites listed within this text are complete with directions and pertinent dive conditions. The easiest way to choose a site is to decide what part of New Jersey you want to visit first. After deciding this, reference the map in front of the book to get the closest sites. Next, read about each site and decide which one meets your dive objectives or experience level. The directions given are from a main thoroughfare so, depending on your location, they might not be the most direct route. Please look at a map to obtain the best possible route; then proceed, following the printed directions in this text.

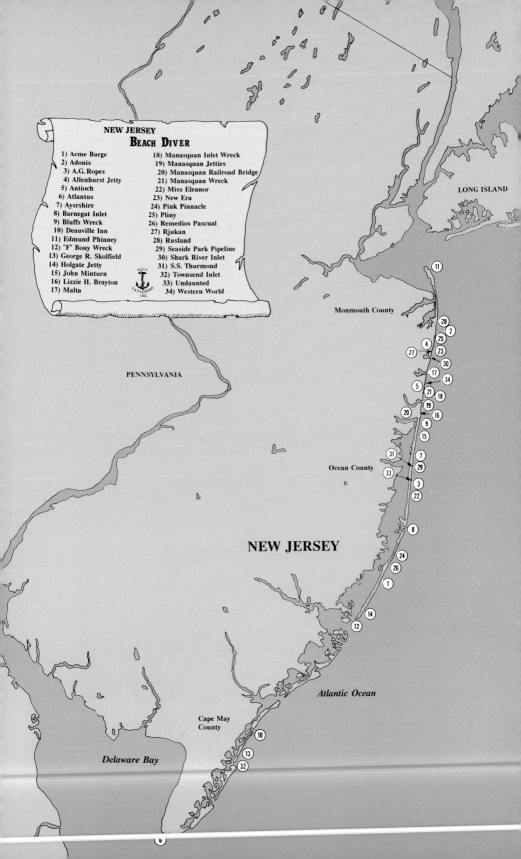

NEW JERSEY
BEACH DIVER

1) Acme Barge
2) Adonis
3) A.G. Ropes
4) Allenhurst Jetty
5) Antioch
6) Atlantus
7) Aysrshire
8) Barnegat Inlet
9) Bluffs Wreck
10) Deauville Inn
11) Edmund Phinney
12) "F" Bouy Wreck
13) George R. Skolfield
14) Holgate Jetty
15) John Minturn
16) Lizzie H. Brayton
17) Malta
18) Manasquan Inlet Wreck
19) Manasquan Jetties
20) Manasquan Railroad Bridge
21) Manasquan Wreck
22) Miss Eleanor
23) New Era
24) Pink Pinnacle
25) Pliny
26) Remedios Pascual
27) Rjukan
28) Rusland
29) Seaside Park Pipeline
30) Shark River Inlet
31) S.S. Thurmond
32) Townsend Inlet
33) Undaunted
34) Western World

LONG ISLAND

Monmouth County

PENNSYLVANIA

Ocean County

NEW JERSEY

Atlantic Ocean

Cape May County

Delaware Bay

Please note that this book is not a complete listing of all New Jersey beach sites. We would like to ask divers to contact the publisher with any additional information so that we may update the text at the next printing.

While reading this book, keep in mind that some locations are known by different names. We have listed most of these names in the index, which is found in the back of the book.

Directions, parking, dive conditions, or even the legality of diving a particular site could change. Please use the information contained within this book only as a basic guideline, and let good diving skills, common sense, and courtesy lead you to enjoy New Jersey's excellent beach diving.

DIVING TIPS

Over the years local beach divers have developed or applied techniques and used certain pieces of equipment to make the sport easier, more enjoyable and safer. Here are a few tips that you might find useful.

SAFETY

A non-diver who comes along for the trip will not only be able to help divers with equipment, but should be informed about the complete dive plan and plan of action if divers do not return on schedule. This beach buddy also should be well informed on all of the diver OK and distress signals.

On remote beaches, a hand-held marine radio or CB will be very useful in the case of an emergency.

Always leave word at home where you will be diving.

A small first aid kit to manage minor cuts and bruises should be assembled and brought on every dive.

SUITING UP

Sand causes the most aggravation to beach divers, as it seems to find the crevices of every piece of equipment such as wet suits, regulators, O rings, etc. To reduce the amount of sand in your gear, either suit up in the car or bring a large plastic tarp to stand on. Another good idea is to bring a bucket and fill it with water before the dive. This way, after finishing your dive, sand can be removed from your feet by stepping into the bucket before stepping back onto the tarp or into your car.

Some wet suits, especially rented ones are often very difficult to get into. One trick

is to mix up a solution of 75% water and 25% liquid soap and keep it readily available in a small squeeze bottle. This solution not only helps divers slip into their suits, but cleans the suit as well.

On cold and windy days, especially while diving in the winter, use your car or other structure as a wind barrier while suiting up or unsuiting.

Bringing a thermos filled with warm water, and pouring some into your gloves or wet suit boots will help take the chill off after a cold water dive. Reusable chemical heat packs also will come in very handy when trying to get rid of a chill.

DIVING

Once in the water, especially when diving a new location, always take a compass bearing straight out from the beach. This basic navigational information allows the diver to swim out and enjoy the dive, while always knowing at least the basic direction the shore is in. Divers can then swim in on a reciprocal course which should bring them back to shore without ever having to surface for directions. Once practiced, this technique should become almost second nature while diving. Another helpful navigational aid is to count the number of kick cycles it takes to swim out. With this count divers then know the approximate number of kick cycles it will take to return to shore, but remember that the kick cycles do not compensate for any changes in current.

If a boat engine is heard while you are submerged, lie flat on the bottom, if possible, next to a big rock until the sound fades. Do not surface to see where the boat is until you are sure it's safe.

A diver can use a flashing light, or tap with the butt of a knife on his own tank to get the attention of his buddy, or other divers. Buddies who dive together should attempt better underwater communications through hand signals or by talking through their regulators. Talking takes some practice, but after awhile you and your buddy will understand what is being said. We have communicated this way in zero visibility when hand signals are of no use.

If you should locate a new wreck, or site that you want to return to, swim to the surface and while staying directly over the site, take compass bearings of two objects that are easily recognizable on the beach. Use objects that are permanent, easy to see, and far enough apart to create about a 90 degree angle.

This double compass course called triangulation is very accurate. If no compass is available, line up two objects on the beach. For example, a telephone pole and the left side of a house. Whatever your land bearings or land ranges are, draw out a little map, and this way, years down the line, you will still be able to find the same spot without having to rely on memory.

When trying to find any of the wrecks off the coast most divers usually find it easier to navigate out with a compass. If the wreck is not located the divers surface to check their land bearings. Recently diver Dan Lieb told us another technique he uses to locate a wreck. Dan recommends swimming out on the surface. The diver holds his dive flag which has a weighted line attached. The weight can be made of sinkers and does not have to be too heavy. While on the surface the diver swims out to the site. Once he passes over the wreck the weighted line bounces and catches into the wreck. The diver then swims down and secures his flag line to the wreck and begins to explore. Dan reports that this method saves on air and allows divers to use land ranges while swimming out to a site.

NIGHT DIVING

Night divers, or any diver for that matter, should never shine a dive light directly into anyone else's eyes. Doing so will ruin or reduce their night vision.

Night diving can be very productive, especially when searching for lobsters. Divers should bring at least two lights plus attach a cylume light stick to their regulator yoke. This chemical light stick enables dive teams to stay in contact with each other by monitoring the cylume light stick's glow.

Navigation back to shore can be made relatively easy by leaving a blinking light similar to a road hazard light on shore before entering the water. This light then gives divers a distinct point to navigate back to after their dive. Believe me, at night the entire coast could look remarkably similar, and this light should prevent some long walks back to your entry point.

UNDERWATER HUNTING

Night is definitely the best time to catch the nocturnal lobster. These tasty crustaceans also can be found during the day by searching through holes that are found in jetties, wrecks, etc. A strong, narrow beam dive light is the best type of light to use when trying to see deep inside these small caves.

Mussels are often ignored by divers in search of dinner, but they shouldn't be, as they are very tasty. Mussels should be collected from mid-water where they are rinsed constantly by the tide and they will be clean and tender. Mussels clinging to poles near the surface in the sunlight will not be as tender, and mussels picked from the bottom will be full of sand or mud.

Spear fishing should only be done in clear water. Always make sure you can see the full distance of your shot. For example, don't use an eight foot cord in four foot visibility, as you could accidentally hit another diver. To spear a fish, swim slowly without making any quick movements, and try for a shot just behind the head. If hit in the stomach, the fish could spin off the spear, while if hit in the head, the spear could just bounce off.

Photo by Jozef Koppelman

EXPLORING NEW DIVE SITES

This book has by no means listed every beach dive in New Jersey. We have listed all the sites which we have knowledge of. There are still miles and miles of unexplored waterfront along the Jersey shore.

The first thing to do when trying to locate a new dive site is to decide on your dive objectives. For example, if you are only interested in catching lobsters, you must look for either rocks, a wreck, a jetty, or some other obstruction where they are known to make their home. If your objective is to find old bottles, a good place to look would be at old fishing piers, or anywhere else that people would drink and discard bottles. If you are interested in underwater photography, you would, of course, want marine life and good visibility.

Let's use the example of a diver who wants to find a new bottling site. The first thing would be to get some old marine charts or maps. You will be amazed at how much information they contain. Look for dump sites, ferry piers, lighthouses, old lifesaving stations etc., and mark them down. Next, look on an up-to-date street map for basic directions. Then you have to do some leg work, and drive to the sites to see if they are accessible. Sometimes there won't be any parking, or a site will be located on private property, but when you do get in the water at a new site, it can be quite rewarding.

To recap, after you pick your dive objective, a little research or planning will usually yield more rewards than trial and error.

TIDES AND CURRENTS

It is extremely important that divers understand the fundamentals before diving in any type of current. Currents are caused by tides, wind, weather and waves. These mass movements of water can sometimes be quite powerful and should not be underestimated.

At most sites divers will encounter a mild tidal current. This might not be to swift, but divers must make a mental note of the general direction so they can compensate when navigating back to shore. Divers also should try to start their dive by swimming into or against any current. This way, at the end of the dive, the current will assist the dive team in returning close to their entry point.

When there is an inlet involved, or whenever a large volume of water is moving through a narrow space during either a Flood or Ebb Tide, the force will be strong. When diving in or around areas that have Rip Currents, divers should realize that the current will disperse after it has passed through the funnel caused by the narrow space. If a diver was to get caught and carried out to sea, it would only be for short distance. A diver who finds himself being carried off should not fight to swim against the current, since this would be a hopeless waste of energy, but should swim parallel to the beach, or across the current, until he gets out of the rip or the current disperses. Then he can easily make his way to the beach without having to fight against the current's force.

Whenever planning a dive in an area that has a strong current, it is best to dive at Slack Tide. Slack Tide simply means that for a short time there is little or no current. Slack occurs in the time lapse when the tide is changing from incoming or outgoing, or from outgoing to incoming. Slack Tide can last from five minutes

Photos by Jozef Koppelman

to two hours, but will usually last for about a half-hour at most New Jersey sites.

The best dives are usually done at High Slack because the incoming flooding tide has just brought in clean ocean water. During Low Slack, the visibility is usually not as good due to the outgoing, Ebbing Tide, which brings out any mud or debris from the inland waterways, especially after a heavy rain.

With the above information in mind, divers should refer to tide tables when planning their dives. Tide tables can be found in most fishing stores or in the daily paper. Make sure the table used is for the correct area since Slack Tide at one location will not occur at the same time as another.

Keep in mind that this is only a brief explanation of tides and currents. For more information, refer to an advanced dive manual, or participate in an advanced diver training course. Remember: plan your dive and dive your plan.

The *Acme Barge* sits in 18 feet of water and is partially exposed at low and high tide.
Photo by Cathie Cush.

ACME BARGE

DIRECTIONS: **(Long Beach Island, Ocean County)**

Take the Garden State Parkway to Exit 63, Rt 72. Stay on Rt 72 over the bridge then drive south on Long Beach Blvd. Continue on Long Beach Blvd to the Acme supermarket in Peahala Park. Make the first right after the supermarket and drive to the end.

CONDITIONS:

The *Acme Barge* was named for its location, behind the Acme supermarket in Peahala Park. According to diver Cathie Cush, the steel barge sits in 18 feet of water, at high tide, and is partially exposed at both low and high tide. Divers can enter the water from the bulkhead. Exits are made easy by using a ladder located on the south end. In an article Cathie wrote about the barge, she reported that "Spring is the best time to dive the barge, because visibility is better." In the summer when the bay water warms up algae reduces visibility. Divers have reported that the barge is covered with bryozoans and tube worms. According to George Dreher, of Triton Divers, be sure to stay close to a Dive Flag as the area is heavily trafficked with pleasure boats and jet skis.

Adonis

The *Adonis* was built in Breman, Germany in 1853, and displaced 550 gross tons. Photo courtesy the author's collection.

The *Adonis* ran aground on March 8, 1859. Her entire crew was taken off by rescuers from lifesaving station number four. Photo Courtesy Mariners Museum, Newport News, Virginia.

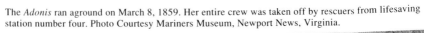

ADONIS

(Long Branch, Monmouth County)
Take the Garden State Parkway to Exit 105 East. Take Rt 36 to the end and turn right on Ocean Ave. Drive south for 2.5 miles, you will see a red church on the right. The retreat house is opposite the church. Note that parking may be a little tricky. I have parked in the dirt lot behind the retreat house on several occasions and have never had a problem. Please remember that this is not public property and divers should use manners, courtesy and good common sense when diving in the area.

CONDITIONS:

The *Adonis* was built in Bremen, Germany in 1853, and displaced 550 gross tons. She was owned by F. Best & Company and valued at $20,000. The *Adonis* was en-route from Newcastle, England to New York, and under the command of Captain Bosse when she struck the beach at 11:00 PM during a heavy fog on March 8, 1859. The wood hulled vessel was carrying a cargo of 124 grindstones, 600 lead ingots, 39 casks of ground flint, 100 casks alkali, 501 casks of soda, 170 casks of powder, 130 casks of carb soda, 200 casks V. red and 500 kegs C. soda.

The *Adonis* wreck is now low lying and scattered.
Photo by Rick Schwarz.

Rick Schwarz (left) and Dan Berg climb down the rock jetty in order to dive the *Adonis*.
Photo by Dan Lieb.

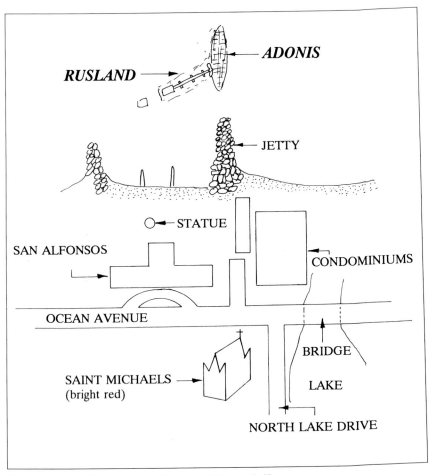

Sketch of the *Dual Wrecks*. Courtesy Patricia and Richard Geffken.

Her entire crew was taken off by rescuers from lifesaving station number four. The wrecking schooners Ringold and Nora were dispatched to the scene. Steam pumps were fitted into the vessels hold to try to reduce the water and re-float the *Adonis* but these efforts were soon abandoned due to rough weather. On March 18th of the same year the vessel broke up in the pounding surf. In the 1960's divers recovered over 300 of the lead ingots she was carrying. Each weighed 115 pounds and had the name Locke Blackett & Co. embossed into them. These early divers also found grindstones ranging in size from two feet to six feet in diameter.

This wreck coupled with the wreck of the *Rusland*, which ran aground on the same spot in 1877, and now sits at a right angle to the *Adonis*, are more commonly known as the *Dual Wrecks*.

Rick Schwarz holds a brass spike and
flange he recovered from the *Adonis*.
Photo by Daniel Berg.

In the 1960's divers recovered over 300
of these lead ingots from the *Adonis*.
Photo courtesy Frank Litter.

Today divers can easily navigate to the *Dual Wrecks*. All that's left of the *Adonis* are low lying wood ribs. Still visible are the remaining five and six foot diameter grindstones and occasionally a diver can recover brass spikes from the site. Howard Rothweiler reports that by digging in the sand just inshore of the grindstones he has located some of her cargo barrels. One barrel contains what appeared to be red dye. The wrecks sit in 25 feet of water and are one of the more interesting beach dives in the area.

A.G. ROPES

DIRECTIONS: **(Island Beach State Park, Ocean County)**
Take the Garden State Parkway to Exit 82 B, Rt 37 East. Stay on Rt 37 over the bridge then bear right at the fork. Continue into Island Beach State Park. Park in section A-12. Park and take path over the dunes.

CONDITIONS:
The three masted schooner *A.G. Ropes* was 258.2 feet long, had a 44.7 foot beam and displaced 2,460 gross tons. She was built in 1884 by Chapman & Ropes in Bath, Maine. In 1906, after a useful life the *A.G. Ropes* was dismasted and sold to Lewis Luckenbach for conversion to a schooner barge. On December 26, 1913, the *A.G. Ropes* and another schooner barge the *Undaunted* were being towed by the tug, Edgar F. Luckenbach. A fierce Christmas gale was blowing and the

The three masted schooner *A.G. Ropes* was 258.2 feet long and had a 44.7 foot beam. Photo courtesy Bill Davis collection.

The *A.G. Ropes* was wrecked on December 26, 1913. Photo courtesy Bill Davis collection.

captain of the tug decided to cut his tow free. He signaled to Captain Olson of the *A.G. Ropes* and Captain Fickett of the *Undaunted* to drop anchor and ride out the storm. Shortly after both barges were washed into the breakers and pounded into pieces. All ten crew members aboard the barges perished.

The wreck of the *A.G. Ropes* now lies buried under a few feet of sand on the beach off Island Beach State Park. The wreck's bow is up by the dunes and her stern is in the surf. After a storm the wreck's outline can be seen in the sand.

ALLENHURST JETTY

DIRECTIONS: (**Allenhurst, Monmouth County**)
Take the Garden State Parkway to Exit 102. Head east on Asbury Ave. Turn left on Main St then right onto Cedar Ave. Take Cedar Ave to the end. Make a Left on Ocean Place. Park and enter through gate. Parking can be a little difficult and a short walk may be required.

CONDITIONS:
The *Allenhurst Jetty*, located just north of Asbury Park is one of the best beach diving locations in the area. Divers should be aware that along the offshore side of the jetty there is sometimes a strong surge. Depth at this site ranges from five to 20

The *Allenhurst Jetty* is one of the best beach dives in the area. Photo by Daniel Berg.

feet. Visibility here is usually pretty good, but the best time to dive the jetty is during high tide. This jetty is known for the abundance of beautiful tropical fish that migrate north with the gulf stream during the summer months. According to Bill Schmoldt, a local diver and shipwreck historian, the best exit is on the inside of the "L" on the south side of the jetty. Bill also reports there may be some wreckage in or near the jetty because some brass artifacts have been located within the jettie's rocks. Bill also tells us that divers can usually find a decent amount of lobsters on the jetty. Diver, Dan Lieb, reports good black fish and excellent night diving on the jetty.

ANTIOCH

DIRECTIONS: (Manasquan, Monmouth County)
Take the Garden State Parkway to Exit 98. Take Rt 34 South straight through two traffic circles. After the second circle take Rt 35 South to Union and turn left, then right onto Main Street. Stay on Main Street to the end and turn left onto First Ave. The wreck is located at the base of Ocean Ave and First Ave.

CONDITIONS:
The *Antioch* was a 180 foot two masted schooner built in 1876. The 986 ton sailing

The *Antioch* was a 180 foot two masted schooner built in 1876. Photo courtesy Gary Gentile.

Lifesavers on the beach worked for twelve hours before successfully transporting all ten crew members to shore. Photo courtesy Daniel Berg collection.

vessel was carrying a cargo of railroad timbers and was en-route from Savannah, Georgia to New York, when she ran aground on March 27, 1914. Captain Morris immediately sent up distress signals. Lifesavers on the beach worked for twelve hours and broke four hawsers before successfully transporting all ten crew members to shore.

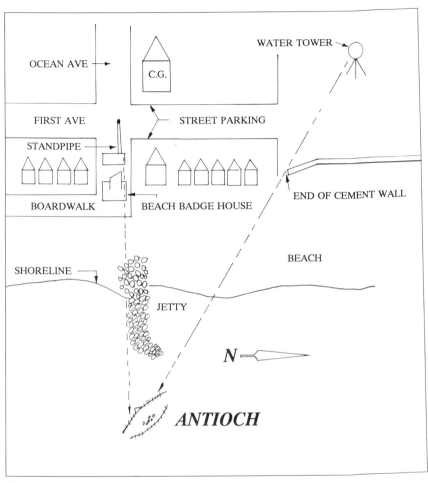

Sketch by Howard Rothweiler.

Diver on the *Antioch*.
Photo by Kevin Brennan.

The wreck lies approximately 150 feet off the end of the jetty. She is resting in 15 to 20 feet of water and lies from east to west. Her bow faces east and there is a pile of anchor chain off the wreck's northeast corner. Diver Bill Schmoldt, reports there are lots of ballast stones on the wreck. Divers also can find a total of three anchors on the site, two on the northeast corner and one just south of the wreck. Please note that this wreck lies low to the bottom and can be a little hard to locate. Visibility ranges from five to over 20 feet at high tide.

ATLANTUS

DIRECTIONS: **(Cape May Point, Cape May County)**
Take the Garden State Parkway south to the end. Travel west on Sunset Boulevard (Route 606) to Sunset Beach. You will come to a parking lot at road's end.

CONDITIONS:
During World War I, while there was a shortage of steel the United States government began to search for alternative materials for ship construction. The *Atlantus* was one of twelve experimental concrete ships. She was built by the Liberty Shipbuilding Co. of Brunswick, Georgia, in their Wilmington, North Carolina shipyard. The *Atlantus* was 250 feet long, had a 43 foot beam and displaced 2,500 tons. She was completed on November 21st and launched on December 4, 1918. The *Atlantus* made several Atlantic crossings, and even

The *Atlantus* was one of twelve experimental concrete ships. Photo courtesy Gary Gentile.

Atlantus

For a while the wreck of the *Atlantus* was used as a bill board. Photo courtesy Bill Davis collection.

Today the deteriorating remains of the concrete ship lie in 20 feet of water, with a slight list to her port side.
Photo by Cathie Cush.

transported soldiers home from France after World I ended. Cathie Cush reported in UNDERWATER USA that, "Although the concrete hulls were more brittle than steel, the concrete ships were less susceptible to vibration from their 1,400 horsepower oil fired steam engines than their steel counterparts." After the war there was not much need for a concrete hulled vessel and the *Atlantus* was removed from service.

In 1920, the *Atlantus* was stripped near Norfolk, Virginia. In 1925 her hull was purchased by the National Navigation Co. The firm was planning to start a ferry service from Cape May, New Jersey to Lewes, Delaware. Elaborate plans were made to beach the *Atlantus* and use her as a ferry terminal. First, a dredge would dig a channel into the beach. The *Atlantus* would be pushed into the channel, and then a gate would be cut into her stern. A ramp would be built for passenger entry and her superstructure removed so her decks could accommodate motor vehicles.

Because of mother nature, these grand plans never became a reality. On June 8, 1926, a storm struck the cape. The *Atlantus* broke free of her mooring and came grounded off Sunset Beach, Cape May. Attempts were made to pull her back into deeper water but they were not successful.

Today, the deteriorating remains of the concrete ship lie in 20 feet of water, with a slight list to her port side. The vessel has broken in half and her superstructure has collapsed. According to Cathie Cush, an avid diver and writer, "On calm days at slack tide, it's possible to swim out to the concrete ship" Cathie goes on to say that, "The site can be deceptive, and both divers and snorklers should approach the wreck with care." Its location at the southern tip of New Jersey puts it near the Mouth of Delaware Bay, making tidal currents a significant consideration. It would be nearly impossible for a diver to swim back to the beach against an outgoing tide." Gary Gentile in his book "SHIPWRECKS OF NEW JERSEY" warns " Approaching the wreck from the water one should also be careful of getting impaled on exposed reinforcing rods that face upward through the waves like punji stakes."

Diver Bill Davis noted on a recent dive that many one and two pound sea bass inhabited the wreckage. Bill also spoke to a fishermen who was anchored to the opposite side of the wreck. The angler had just caught a striped bass and reported that he often catches stripers, blues, weakfish and flounder around the wreck.

AYSRSHIRE

DIRECTIONS: **(Seaside Heights, Ocean County)**
Note: The Location of this wreck site is presently un-known.

CONDITIONS:
The Scottish Brig *Aysrshire* foundered off Seaside Heights on January 12, 1850. At the time she was carrying 201 English and Irish immigrants. When this wreck went up on the beach lifesavers used the lifesaving gun to haul a line over her. From this line a stronger rope was hauled to the wreck. This was the first time this type of equipment was ever used and all passengers and crew were safely transported to the beach.

To the best of my knowledge, no one is presently diving on this wreck. With a little research and some exploratory dives the *Aysrshire* should not be to difficult to locate.

BARNEGAT INLET

DIRECTIONS: **(Island Beach State Park, Ocean County)**
Note: A four-wheel-drive vehicle and permit are needed to access this site.
Take the Garden State Parkway to Exit 82 B, Rt 37 East. Stay on Rt 37 over the bridge then bear right at the fork. Continue into Island Beach State Park. Continue to the end.

Photo courtesy Herb & Veronica Segars.

CONDITIONS:

Barnegat Inlet is located in central New Jersey. Diving, however, is not permitted from the south side of the inlet. To dive the north side of the inlet you must enter from the beach at Island Beach State Park. Access to the area requires a beach permit and a four wheel drive vehicle.

Due to the conditions here, diving this inlet is a challenge and should be considered an advanced dive. Visibility is often poor due to the strong current and stirred up sediment from summer boat traffic. Current regulations require buddy teams, a dive flag and state that divers must surface within 25 feet of their flag. Due to the high concentration of boat traffic, it is highly recommended to stay close to the rocks and out of the main channel.

Located inside the inlet beyond where the channel turns south are the remains of a World War II submarine net. This steel net had been stretched across the inlet in an effort to keep German submarines out of the bay. The counter weight, track and net are lying in the sand in approximately 20 feet of water. Mussels now cover the nets making them barely visible.

BLUFFS WRECK

Even though never positively identified many believe this wreck to be the *Creole*, a coastal steamer built in 1862. Photo courtesy Gary Gentile.

Bluffs Wreck

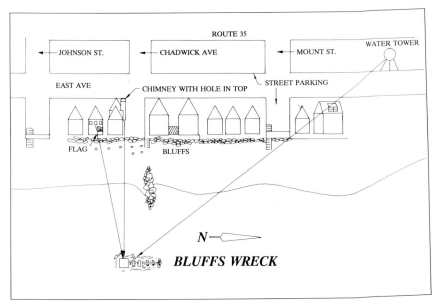

Sketch by Howard Rothweiler.

DIRECTIONS: (Bay Head, Ocean County)

Take the Garden State Parkway to Exit 98. Take Rt 34, you will pass through two traffic circles. After the second circle Rt 34 will change into Rt 35. Continue over the bridge to the end and turn left on to Sea Ave. Take Sea Ave to Ocean Ave and turn right. Head South to Mount Street and turn left.

CONDITIONS:

The *Bluffs Wreck* is a favorite check out site for diving instructors. The wreck is located in 20 feet of water 200 feet off the jetty in Bay Head. On the wreck divers will find steel hull plates, boilers and machinery. This wreck was named after the hotel that was located here for years. This hotel was just recently replaced with a restaurant. The wreck's true identity still remains a mystery. Although sometimes called the *Creole*, no positive identification has yet been made. Even though never positively identified, this wreck's description is consistent with that of the steamer *Creole*, a coastal steamer built in 1862.

According to Bill Davis, the south end of the wreck is dominated by a large rectangular boiler and is home to various species of fish. Black fish up to seven pounds have been taken by spear fishermen. As you swim north on the wreckage you come to an area with large machinery. From this area Bill and his dive buddies recovered a brass capstan, but unfortunately it did not bear any markings or give any additional clues about the wreck's name.

Continuing north the wreckage disappears into the sand leaving only her propeller shaft exposed. Swimming along the propeller shaft, debris will be noticed off the wreck. This area is well worth exploring as bottles and a few American coins have been found here.

Swimming off the wreck out towards the east are the large remains of her decking. This area is a great spot not only to look for artifacts but for lobsters as well. At times this decking can be completely covered over by the shifting sands.

DEAUVILLE INN

DIRECTIONS: (Strathmere, Cape May County)
Take the Garden State Parkway to Exit 17, Sea Isle Blvd. Stay on Sea Isle, Rt 625 to Landis Ave and turn left. Landis will turn into Common Wealth Ave. The Deauville Inn will be on the left side just before the bridge.

CONDITIONS:
Located in Strathmere, a stones throw from Ocean City is the *Deauville Inn* restaurant. The dive area received its name from the restaurant, which is the only noticeable land mark near Corson's Inlet.

Sketch by Dave Keller.

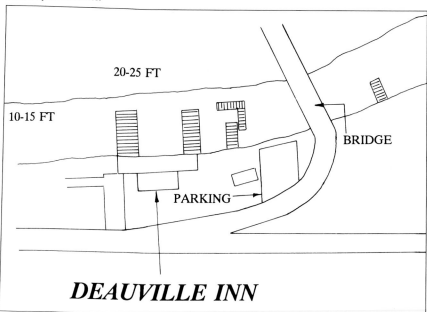

20-25 FT

10-15 FT

BRIDGE

PARKING

DEAUVILLE INN

Deauville Inn

This dive site received its name from the restaurant. Photo by Dolores Rothweiler.

This area is well known for recovering bottles and is considered the premier bottle dive of south Jersey. Photo courtesy Dave Keller.

Currently Corson's Inlet is considered closed to navigation, although you get an occasional boater attempting to traverse the area.

The area is well known for recovering bottles and is considered the premier bottle dive of south Jersey. Bottles are easily recovered and many times are above the sand. After a quick survey of the area if you don't locate any bottles on top of the sand, just pick an area and start fanning. At times divers will find bottles in piles, but sometimes you have to move frequently and dig to find anything. According to diver Dave Keller, bottles recovered here date back from the mid 1800's to the prohibition era. Divers have also recovered jewelry, coins, china, and silverware at the site.

The marine life at the site is abundant and includes lobsters, crabs, flounder, skates, shrimp, coral, mussels and clams. Depth ranges from ten to 25 feet with visibility between two and 20 feet. The best time to dive this site is during high slack and in the winter, spring or fall. Dave also tells us that the currents and summer boat traffic are the area's main hazards.

EDMUND PHINNEY

View of the shore from directly over the *Edmund Phinney* wreck. Courtesy Frank Litter.

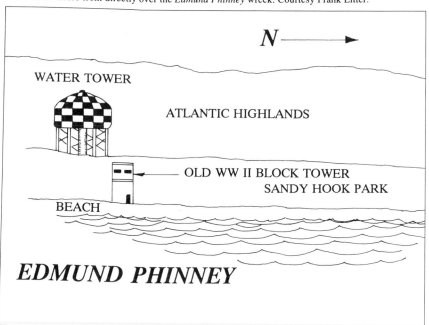

N

WATER TOWER

ATLANTIC HIGHLANDS

OLD WW II BLOCK TOWER
SANDY HOOK PARK

BEACH

EDMUND PHINNEY

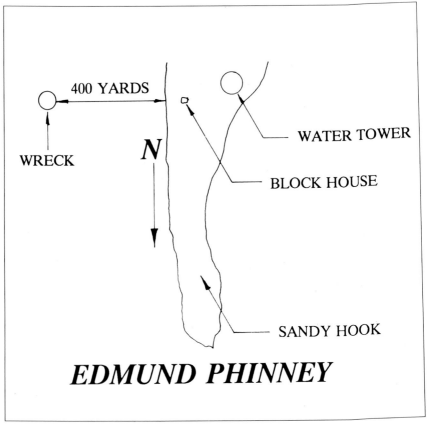

Sketch by Frank Litter.

DIRECTIONS: **(Sandy Hook, Monmouth County)**
Note: Although it may be possible to swim to this wreck from the beach it is highly recommended to only access this site by boat.

CONDITIONS:
The bark *Edmund Phinney* ran aground during a fierce 70 mile per hour gale on December 14, 1907. She had originally struck shore opposite the Sandy Hook Lifesaving Station about three quarters of a mile offshore. While lifesavors on the beach made one unsuccessful attempt at towing a life boat to the stricken vessel the *Phinney* drifted to within 400 yards of the beach. A shot line was fired over the wreck and her crew secured it to the mizzens lower mast and then hauled out the hawser lines. All of the *Phinney's* crew were rescued and with no time wasted. In fact, according to the book BROKEN SPARS, "Just as the master and the mate of the *Edmund Phinney* touched shore, the bark crumpled and fell into the sea."

Frank Litter displays a dead eyes he recovered from the *Edmund Phinney*.

Dead eye from the *Edmund Phinney*. Photo by Frank Litter.

According to diver Frank Litter, the *Edmund Phinney* is also called the *Dead Eye Wreck*. The wreck is inverted in approximately 25 feet of water about 400 yards off the beach at Sandy Hook. Divers have recovered dozens of dead eyes, brass spikes, blocks, bottles and the ship's anchor that weighed about a ton. The anchor was a wood stock type. This wreck covers over with sand frequently which makes locating the site a little tricky.

"F" BUOY WRECK

DIRECTIONS: **(Long Beach Island, Atlantic County)**
Note: This site is only accessible by boat.
This wreck sits 200 yards southeast of Tuckers Island, which is located in Beach Haven Inlet just south of Long Beach Island.

CONDITIONS:
Located approximately 100 feet southwest of the *"F" Buoy* near the Little Egg Inlet are the scattered remains of a wooden vessel believed to be an old sailing ship. Although her name or origin is not known to divers, she is well known to those fishermen who have lost rigs while drifting over the site.

The wreckage can be easily identified by using a depth recorder. She sits in 28 feet of water and rises five feet off the bottom. Her wooden remains are scattered over 150 feet of sandy bottom. There are many fishing rigs and lures around the wreck site so divers should be careful. Small bait fish as well as stripped bass and bluefish are common and it's not uncommon to see lobster, although they are mostly small.

In her wooden planks brass spikes of various sizes still hold decking together. Two large wooden masts can be found amidships. No heavy machinery has been located, therefore it is our belief that the wreck has been salvaged.

Although it may be possible to swim to the wreck from Tucker's Island it is not advisable due to the current and boat traffic. As a matter of fact, it is best only to dive this site during the winter months and at slack tide. Visibility is dictated by weather and tides, and when conditions are right visibility can be 30 feet.

GEORGE R. SKOLFIELD

DIRECTIONS: **(Sea Isle City, Cape May County)**
Take the Garden State Parkway to Exit 17 N. Stay on Sea Isle Blvd until over the bridge, then turn right onto Landis Ave. The wreck is off Landis Ave.

CONDITIONS:
The three masted schooner, *George R. Skolfield* was built in 1885 by George R. Skolfield in Brunswick, Maine. She was 232 feet long, had a 39 foot beam and displaced 1,728 gross tons.

The three masted schooner, *George R. Skolfield* was built in 1885. Photo courtesy Bill Davis collection.

The *George R. Skolfield* was 232 feet long and had a 39 foot beam.
Photo courtesy The Bath Marine Museum.

On February 5, 1920, the *Skolfield*, which had been converted into a barge, broke free from her tow and drifted onto the beach. Photo courtesy Gary Gentile.

On February 5, 1920, the *Skolfield*, which had been converted into a schooner barge, broke free from her tow. The *Skolfield* drifted until becoming stranded on Ludlum Beach, Sea Isle City. Lifesavors from the beach launched a surf boat and despite the huge waves were successful in rescuing and taking her four crewmen safely ashore.

Today, the scattered wreck is found in only five feet of water. During low tide some wreckage protrudes above the ocean's surface. Her shallow depth coupled with the fact that most of the wreck is buried under the sand, make the *George R. Skolfield* undesirable to most divers.

HOLGATE JETTY

DIRECTIONS: **(Holgate, Ocean County)**
Take the Garden State Parkway to Exit 63, Rt 72. Stay on Rt 72 over the bridge, then turn right on Long Beach Blvd. Drive south into Holgate.

CONDITIONS:
Most the jetties along Long Beach Island or for that matter the New Jersey coast are productive for divers who want to hunt for lobsters and crabs or for spear fisherman looking for black fish. The *Holgate Jetty* is the largest of these jetties on Long Beach Island and therefore provides area divers better opportunities to bring home dinner. According to diver Cathie Cush, the *Holgate Jetty* is constructed of large cement blocks and rocks. The jetty is longer than it appears on the surface and as you move away from the beach the structure becomes submerged.

JOHN MINTURN

DIRECTIONS: **(Mantoloking, Ocean County)**
Take the Garden State Parkway to Exit 98, Rt 34 South. Stay on Rt 34 straight through two traffic circles. After the second circle take Rt 35. After two lane highway reduces to a single lane turn right on Princeton Ave. Wreck is off Princeton Ave. Please note that there is no close parking available.

CONDITIONS:
The sailing vessel *John Minturn*, under the command of Captain Starke, ran aground at 8:00 AM during a fierce gale on February 14, 1856. This storm became known as the "Great Northeast Snowstorm of 1846" and was responsible for the loss of at least ten vessels and 60 lives. The beaches of Monmouth County were

The *John Minturn* ran aground during a fierce gale on February 14, 1856. Photo Daniel Berg collection.

strewn with ships' cargo and human bodies for days. Unfortunately for those aboard the *John Minturn*, they had suffered the greatest loss of life. Due to the turbulent sea, nothing could be done to rescue the 51 passengers and crew trapped on the doomed ship. Finally, at 10:00 PM, after a gruelling day the *John Minturn* broke apart. Passengers' cries could be heard as the vessel dumped them into the freezing sea. Only a handful of survivors were picked out of the ocean and brought to safety. According to the book "PERILS OF THE PORT OF NEW YORK" by Jeannette Rattray "A New York pilot, Thomas Freeborne, was on board. Freeborne gave his coat to the captain's wife, who was on board with her children." He then froze to death. "A monument was erected in Greenwood Cemetery, Brooklyn, as a testimonial to Thomas Freeborne's self-sacrifice." In all, 42 passengers and crew members died, and although Mr. Freeborne's actions were heroic, Captain Stark, his wife and children were included in the fatalities.

Today, the unidentified wreck known as *John Minturn* lies just beyond the surf off Mantoloking, New Jersey. The wood wreck sits in 20 feet of water.

LIZZIE H. BRAYTON

DIRECTIONS: **(Point Pleasant, Monmouth County)**
Take the Garden State Parkway to Exit 98, Rt 34. After driving thought the second traffic circle Rt 34 will change into Rt 35. Continue over the bridge into Point

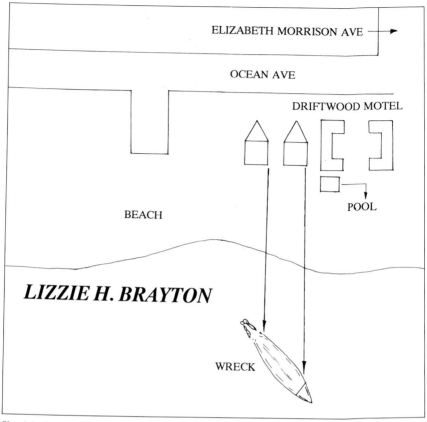

Sketch by Howard Rothweiler.

Pleasant. Make a left hand "U" turn immediately after bridge, then a quick right onto Broadway. Take Broadway to the end and turn right onto Ocean Ave. Stay on Ocean for approximately three miles. The wreck is directly in front of the Driftwood Motel, which will be on the left side.

CONDITIONS:

The *Lizzie H. Brayton* was a 201 foot, 979 ton, four masted schooner. She was built in 1891 at Bath, Maine. At 2:00 AM on December 18, 1904, the *Brayton* while en-route from Lamberts Point, Virginia to New Haven, Connecticut, with a cargo of coal struck a sand bar during a fierce snow storm. With the assistance of the surfmen at the Bay Head Lifesaving Station, the crew of nine was successfully rescued in breeches buoys. A few days after the *Lizzie H. Brayton* came ashore a storm blew up and swamped the stranded vessel.

The wreck lies in ten to 15 feet of water 160 yards off Point Pleasant, and can be

The *Lizzie H. Brayton* ran aground on December 18, 1904. Photo courtesy Daniel Berg collection.

located by swimming directly east from the Driftwood Motel. The wreck lies north to south. Diver, Bill Schmoldt, reports that this wreck is easy to locate due to her high profile and that divers will still be able to see a disturbance in the waves directly over the wreck at low tide.

This wreck was relocated and identified by divers Carlos Narciso, Tom Nolan and Howard Rothweiler in March of 1990. Howard reports that "When we first

Sketch of the *Lizzie H. Brayton*. Courtesy Tom Nolan.

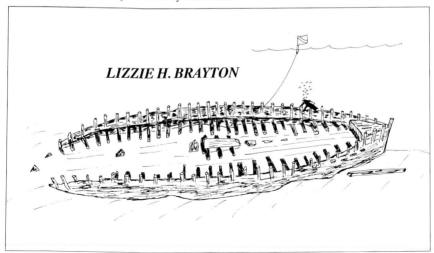

LIZZIE H. BRAYTON

discovered the wreck, it arose from the sand only about five feet at its' highest point. When I returned in December of 1991, much more of the vessel was showing. Near the bow section, the side of the ship sticks up at least seven feet. The inside is filled with about two feet of sand. About half way back toward the stern the wreck begins to break up and disappear into the sand, only to reappear 20 feet further back." Howard also reports that divers will find coal scattered around the site.

MALTA

DIRECTIONS: (Belmar, Monmouth County)
Take the Garden State Parkway to Exit 100 and head east on Rt 33. Turn right on Main St, then left on 9th Ave. The wreck is off Ocean Ave at the base of 9th.

Sketch on the *Malta* wreck area. Sketch courtesy Patricia and Richard Geffken.

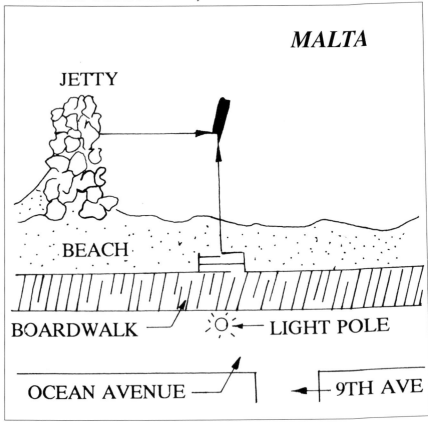

Photo of *Malta* wreck site. Look closely and you can see her rudder post protruding through the surface. Photo by Howard Rothweiler.

CONDITIONS:

The *Malta* was originally built in 1852 as the *Queen Of The South*. She was then re-named *Milford Haven*. In the early 1870's she was converted to sail and renamed *Malta*. The *Malta* was 244 feet long, had a 40 foot beam and displaced 1,600 tons.

The *Malta* was en-route from Antwerp to New York with thousands of empty petroleum barrels. At 3:30 AM November 24, 1855, the *Malta* ran aground during a fierce northeast gale. Within minutes of running aground the surfmen from the nearby Lifesaving Station came to the rescue and attempted to shoot a rescue line across the bow of the stricken vessel. On the third try, the crew aboard the *Malta* caught the line and secured it twenty feet up the foremast. Lifesavers used a breeches buoy to rescue 23 of the 24 crew. One sailor apparently delirious with fear attempted to swim to shore rather than waiting for his turn on the breeches buoy. His body was found six miles away the next day.

Photo courtesy Herb & Veronica Segars.

After many futile attempts to pull the *Malta* into deeper water the ship finally gave in to the constant pounding of the surf and broke amidships on December 11, 1885.

Today, the wreckage of the steamer lies about 100 yards off the beach in 20 feet of water. Visibility around the wreck ranges from one to 15 feet. The *Malta's* cargo included wood barrels, some of which can still be observed on the site. According to Bill Davis, the exposed section of the wreck is metal and measures approximately ten feet by five feet wide. Her anchor can still be seen rising from the sand off the wreck, but is often overlooked due to the marine growth that disguises it. Diver Bill Schmoldt tells us that her rudder was standing up for years and that not too many artifacts have been recovered from the site, probably because most the wreck is always buried.

No diving is permitted off the shore here between 9:00 AM and 5:00 PM from Memorial Day to Labor Day. Best conditions are at high tide and divers should wait for a calm day. Captain Kevin Brennan reports that at low tide her rudder post protrudes through the surface, which makes locating the wreck site simple.

MANASQUAN INLET WRECK

DIRECTIONS: **(Manasquan, Monmouth County)**
Take the Garden State Parkway to Exit 98. Take Rt 34 South, you will pass straight through two traffic circles. After the second circle get on Rt 35 South. Turn left onto Union Ave, then right onto Fisk Ave. Fisk will turn into Brielle Rd. Stay on Brielle Rd to the end and turn right onto First Ave.

CONDITIONS:
A few years back divers Tom Nolan and Carlos Narciso were planning to dive the *Manasquan Wreck*. While trying to locate the wreckage they were carried southeast by a current. In attempting a search pattern they came across a small wooden wreck in 27 feet of water. Thinking this was a newly uncovered piece of the *Manasquan Wreck*, they investigated intensely until they ran low on air. The divers took land ranges and when they compared them to the land ranges for the *Manasquan Wreck*, they discovered they were quite distant.

On their next trip to the wreck, accompanied by Howard Rothweiler, the divers explored the new wreck to see if they could identify any similarities between this site and the *Manasquan Wreck*. Finding no conclusive evidence, but finding many differences in wood shape and size, the team believes tne two sites to be of different wrecks. For lack of a better name this site has become known as the *Manasquan Inlet Wreck* or *Barge Wreck*.

Carlos Narciso holds two spikes he recovered from the *Manasquan Inlet Wreck*. Photo by Daniel Berg.

Today divers will find wooden ribs held together with brass pins and large steel cubes that may have been used for ballast or trade. Carlos reports that the wreck site is approximately 200 feet long and almost 100 feet wide. Although no artifacts recovered positively identify the wreck, some believe she is the wreck of the *Civita Carrera*.

MANASQUAN JETTIES

DIRECTIONS: **(Manasquan/Pt Pleasant, Monmouth County)**
Take the Garden State Parkway to Exit 98. Take Rt 34 South, you will go straight through two traffic circles. After the second traffic circle get on to Rt 35 South. After crossing the Manasquan River make a left hand "U" turn, then a quick right onto Broadway. Stay on Broadway to the end and turn left onto Ocean Ave.

CONDITIONS:
The *Manasquan Jetties* are excellent not only for underwater photography but for lobster, black fish, crabs and even striped bass. The best dive conditions are at

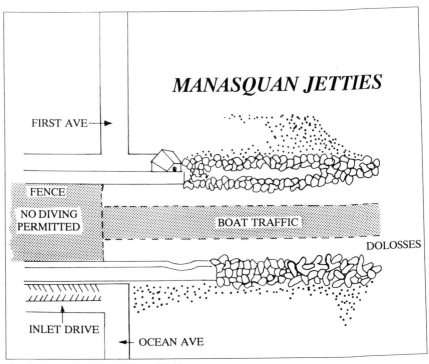

MANASQUAN JETTIES

FIRST AVE

FENCE
NO DIVING
PERMITTED

BOAT TRAFFIC

DOLOSSES

INLET DRIVE

OCEAN AVE

Sketch courtesy Patricia and Richard Geffken

Photos courtesy Herb &
Veronica Segars

44

high slack. The site does have several regulations, but the benefits are well worth adhering to them. First, diving is only permitted within 50 feet of the jetties or bulkheads. Second, diving is only permitted east of an imaginary line drawn from Ocean Ave to First Ave (refer to diagram). Since regulations may change it is recommended to contact local municipalities to check on up dates. Divers also should realize that boat traffic through the inlet at this location is heavy and divers are urged, for their own safety, to stay near the rocks. Diver Bill Schmoldt tells us that over the years a few small boats have gone aground on the jetties. The current quickly washes the little wrecks away or rips apart the wreckage and leaves little remaining, but who knows what souvenirs can be found by observant divers.

MANASQUAN RIVER RAILROAD BRIDGE

DIRECTIONS: (Point Pleasant, Monmouth County)
Take the garden State Parkway to Exit 98, Rt 34 South. Take Rt 34 straight through two traffic circles. After the second circle get on Rt 35 South. After crossing the Manasquan River bridge get over into the left lane and follow the signs for "Broadway Beach Area." You will make a left side "U" turn, then a quick right onto Broadway. Once on Broadway the you will see a small parking lot to

The *Railroad Bridge* is a great dive for both beginners and experienced alike. Photo by Daniel Berg.

the left. The dive site is located directly across from the 7-11 conveniece store on Broadway in Point Pleasant.

CONDITIONS:

The *Manasquan River Railroad Bridge* in Point Pleasant is a great dive for both beginners and experienced alike. This site offers depths up to 25 feet and consistent diving conditions. You can almost always depend on calm and clear water.

The dive site can be divided into two sites. Identified by either the bayside and oceanside of the railroad bridge. On the bayside divers often observe seahorse, eels, sponges and fluke. On the oceanside where there is a current, bluefish, fluke and stripped bass can be found. Around the railroad bridge itself are the remains of the original railroad bridge that collapsed into the river over 100 years ago.

The original bridge was built out of red brick from the Joseph Brick foundry (Bricktown, NJ, was later named after Joseph Brick). Some of the recovered brick still has the family shield on it. This dive site is also known as *Gull Island County Park*. It is recommended to dive here at slack tide, preferably high slack. The bottom is sand and mud. Please also note the boat traffic and dive safely. As a side note two portholes have been found while diving this site. This may indicate that a wreck is in the area. Captain Kevin Brennan reports that off *Gull Island Park* in 15 feet of water are the remains of old pilings and timbers from a wreck. Howard Rothweiler reports that many round bottom bottles have been recovered from this site. These bottles may be from one of the sailing vessels that docked in the area due to deep water or they may have come from people on the train, discarding them through a window as they rode along. Howard also reports that several large propellers and a brass rudder were recovered from the area.

MANASQUAN WRECK

DIRECTIONS: (Manasquan, Monmouth County)

Take the Garden State Parkway to Exit 98. Take Rt 34 South, you will pass straight through two traffic circles. After the second circle get on Rt 35 South. Turn left onto Union Ave, then right onto Fisk Ave. Fisk will turn into Brielle Rd. Stay on Brielle Rd to the end and turn right onto First Ave. The wreck is located just south of Pompano Ave.

CONDITIONS:

The *Manasquan Wreck* sits in 30 feet of water and lies 300 yards offshore and

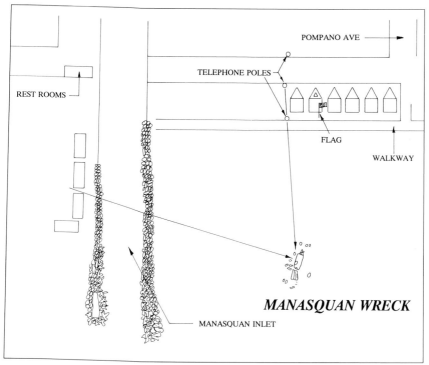

MANASQUAN WRECK

Sketch by Howard Rothweiler.

1,000 feet north of Manasquan Inlet. She appears to be the remains of an old English sailing ship. Her stern is facing shore and it's very easy to miss the wreck when trying to navigate to her from the beach. The stern section is about 30 feet long. Dan Lieb reports that loads of artifacts are found on this site.

This wreck is rumored to be the privateer *Thistle*, which was sunk in 1813. Due to the assortment of artifacts found here, she is also nick-named the *Rickel Wreck*, after the chain of hardware stores. Diver Frank Litter who explored this wreck back in the early 1960's told me that divers also used to call it the *Hardware Wreck* or *Barrel Wreck*. Frank went on to say that he had recovered some pewter spoons from one of her cargo barrels labeled "T. Hill" which is a British manufacturer. The spoons were made for only one year 1846 to 1847. The dates on Frank's spoons would seem to rule out the possibilities of this wreck actually being the *Thistle*. I have heard various rumors of a cannon located in the area of the wreck, which may indicate upon investigation that the *Thistle* is located close by. My friend Bill Schmoldt who also does not think that this wreck is the *Thistle* says he knows of at least one diver who has found a cannon ball near the wreck. Bill believes that the *Manasquan Wreck* may be the remains of the *Elizabeth*, or

Manasquan Wreck

Carlos Narciso returning from a dive to the *Manasquan Wreck*. Photo by Howard Rothweiler.

Barrels containing the wreck's cargo can still be found on the site. Photo by Kevin Brennan.

Tom Nolan with rudder recovered in the area of the *Manasquan Wreck*. Photo courtesy Howard Rothweiler.

Silverware and a black glass "case gin" bottle from the *Manasquan Wreck*. Photo by Frank Litter.

Diver Ed Maliszewski recovered these artifacts from the *Manasquan Wreck*. Photo by Daniel Berg.

Pen knives and files recovered from the *Manasquan Wreck*.
Photo by Howard Rothweiler.

From left to right, David Schwartzman, Rob Davillary and Frank Kenny with a barrel filled with farming hoe heads. Photo by Ramona Davillary.

the *San Juan*. Another diver Dave Schwartzman, lifted one of the barrels from the wreck and found it to contain hoe heads for farming. Other artifacts recovered include knife handles, draw handles, disassembled flint locks, silver bells, brass pots, buttons, chains, wire, buckles and pewter. This wreck is better to dive from a boat but many do choose to make the swim from the beach.

MISS ELEANOR

DIRECTIONS: **(Island Beach State Park, Ocean County)**
Take the Garden State Parkway to Exit 82 B, Rt 37 East. Stay on Rt 37 over the bridge then bear right at the fork. Continue into Island Beach State Park. Parking

Sketch of the *Miss Eleanor* wreck site. Courtesy Howard Rothweiler.

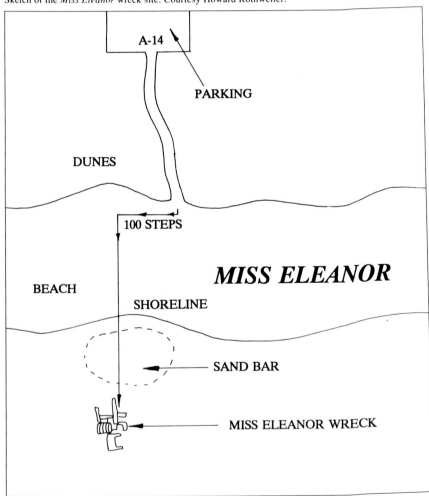

Dolores Rothweiler next to wreckage from the *Miss Eleanor*. The wreck can be seen in the background. Photo by Howard Rothweiler.

in section A-14, walk on the path over the dunes. The wreck is located 100 feet to the right of the path and approximately 150 feet offshore.

Howard Rothweiler holds the name plaque he recovered from the wreck. Photo by Daniel Berg.

On January 4, 1988, the clam dredge *Miss Eleanor* developed a severe leak when her dredge smashed through her wooden hull. Captain Russell Stump immediately radioed a distress call. The captain, in an effort to save his vessel and crew, then steamed for the beach. He wanted to intentionally run the *Miss Eleanor* aground in the shallow water off Island Beach State Park. After running aground all three crew members were successfully rescued. Any plans to salvage the *Miss Eleanor* were abandoned when the constant pounding from the surf split the vessel at her seams. Within a few days the vessel was splintered apart and pieces of debris littered the beach.

Today the wreck protrudes through the surf in seven feet of water. The wreck consists of her main beam and heavy machinery. Those who want to dive the wreck should park in area A-14, walk to the beach, and look for her remains above the surf. As with most Jersey beach sites divers should wait for a calm day to explore this site.

NEW ERA

DIRECTIONS: **(Deal, Monmouth County)**
Note: The exact location of this wreck is presently unknown. Although a few divers claim to know the wrecks location, it remains a well kept secret.

CONDITIONS:
The three masted German packet *New Era* ran aground during a storm on the evening of November 13, 1854. Of the 415 passengers who boarded the *New Era* in Bremen, Germany, 43 had already died from cholera. Frustrated rescuers on the beach could only get close enough to the ship to hear the anguished cries for help. Finally, the next morning lifesavors were able to reach the wreck. They untied a young boy who had been lashed to her mast. Around him hung arms and legs lashed fast from which the bodies had been torn away. Only 132 survived the calamity and 240 died from exposure and drowning.

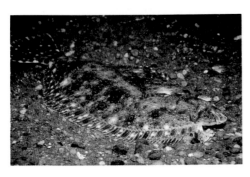

Photo courtesy Herb & Veronica Segars.

PINK PINNACLE

DIRECTIONS: **(Surf City, Ocean County)**
Take the Garden State Parkway to Exit 63, Rt 72 East. Stay on Rt 72 over the bridge then turn left on Long Beach Blvd. Continue into the town of Surf City. The wreck is off Seventh Street beach.

CONDITIONS:
This unidentified wooden shipwreck was named the *Pink Pinnacle* by local divers who noticed a pinkish marine growth on the wreck. The wreck appears to be the remains of a wooden schooner from the late 1800's. Cathie Cush reported in an UNDERWATER USA article that the schooner "was supposed to have carried fertilizer."

The wreck lies 125 feet off the beach in 18 to 22 feet of water and can be located by taking a 180 degree compass course from the third house north of the beach entrance at Seventh Street. If you reach 25 feet of water you have missed the wreck. The 100 foot long wreck sits upright and parallel to the beach. Her gunwales and her bow sprit are all that remain unburied.

There has been some speculation that the *Pink Pinnacle* is actually the wreck of the *Powhattan*. The *Powhattan* was a three masted packet ship that ran aground in April of 1854. Unfortunately, to date no one to my knowledge has recovered an artifact that would positively identify this wreck.

PLINY

DIRECTIONS: **(Deal, Monmouth County)**
Take the Garden State Parkway to Exit 105. Take Rt 36 until the traffic circle. At the circle get on Rt 32, Wall St. Take Rt 32 to Monmouth Rd and turn right. Turn left on Cedar Ave and take it to the d. Turn right on Ocean Ave and head south. Turn right on Phillips Ave and park. The wreck is located directly in front of Deal Casino.

CONDITIONS:
The British cargo ship *Pliny* was built by Barrow Ship Builders Company of England in 1878. She was 288.4 feet long, had a 33.3 foot beam and displaced 1,671 gross tons. The *Pliny* was owned by Liverpool, Brazil & River Plate Company and was powered by compound inverted engines.

Pliny

The British cargo ship *Pliny* was built by Barrow Ship Builders Company of England in 1878. She was 288.4 feet long, had a 33.3. foot beam and displaced 1,671 gross tons. Photo courtesy The Mariners Museum, Newport News, Virginia.

On May 13, 1882, the *Pliny* ran aground during a fierce storm. Photo courtesy The Mariners Museum, Newport News, Virginia.

THE WRECK OF THE "PLINY" AT DEAL BEACH, NEW JERSEY, SATURDAY, MAY 13.—From Sketches by Theo. R. Davis.—[See Page 327.]

54

Diver Dan Lieb points the way to the *Pliny* wreck. Photo by Daniel Berg.

On April 22, 1882, the *Pliny* left Rio De Janeiro with a general cargo of 20,000 bags of coffee, 300 bales of hides, 21 passengers and 34 crew. On May 13, the schooner rigged vessel ran aground during a fierce storm. The Lifesaving Service quickly assembled and rescued all passengers and crew. Operations to remove the *Pliny's* cargo continued until May 16th, when the *Pliny* broke in two. According to diver and shipwreck historian, Bill Davis, "It was discovered later that a passenger had $3,000 in gold coins locked up in the safe of the captain's cabin. It is assumed that this safe was never recovered."

Sketch of the *Pliny* wreck area. Courtesy Howard Rothweiler.

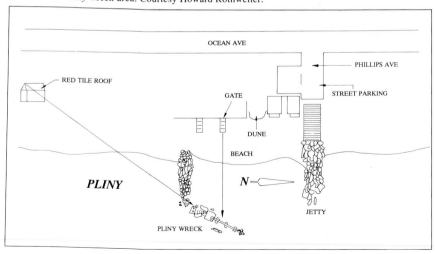

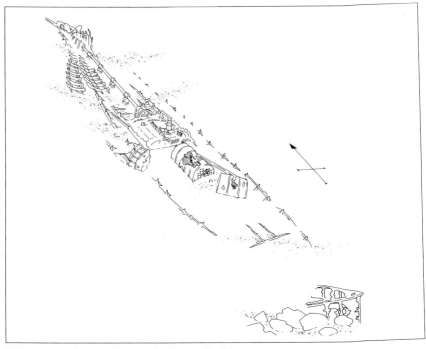

Underwater sketch of the *Pliny* wreck. Courtesy Dan Lieb.

The wreck now rests in ten to 25 feet of water, about 200 yards out, directly in front of the Deal Casino Beach Club. According to diver, Dan Lieb, the wreck is half buried in the sand and lies with her bow pointing south. Her stern is covered in seaweed. Her rudder post plus her propeller remain easily recognizable. Dan goes on to report that her flywheel has spokes large enough to swim through. Although the *Pliny* is not well known for recovering artifacts, in the bow of the wreck divers can find brass spikes from her wooden decking. Bill Schmoldt reports there is a five foot fluted anchor on the eastern side of the wreck. Bill Davis reports that the

Dan Berg uses a propulsion unit to make the swim off shore a little easier. Photo by Jozef Koppelman.

north side of the wreckage consists of a long propeller shaft held up off the sand by steel and brass supports. Midships are her engine and other related equipment. Diver, Howard Rothweiler reports that large black fish inhabit this wreck, and in the past he has speared some in excess of ten pounds.

REMEDIOS PASCUAL

DIRECTIONS: **(Shipbottom, Ocean County)**
Take the Garden State Parkway to Exit 63, Rt 72. Continue on Rt 72 over the bridge then take Long Beach Blvd north to 7th Street east. Go to the end, park and walk two houses over to the north. Swim due east for 100 yards.

CONDITIONS:

The *Remedios Pascual* was built by J. Urquhart Barton, of Nova Scotia in 1885. She was originally named the *Stalwart*, was 216 feet long, had a 40 foot beam and displaced 1,605 gross tons.

On October 18, 1902, the schooner, under the command of Captain Tablo Ganto, left Buenos Aires en-route for New York, transporting a cargo of animal bones to a fertilizer factory. The journey should have taken approximately 50 days but due to alternating light winds and heavy storms, the journey took longer.

On January 3, 1903, the *Pascual* entered thick fog. Before long she was aground on Ship Bottom Bars. Keeper Truex of Lifesaving Station #20 spotted the vessel in distress and summoned his crew to render assistance. The lifesavers on the beach fired two lines over the stranded ship, but the sailors on the *Pascual* were too frightened and did not haul the breeches buoy tackle aboard. The lifesavers then launched a lifeboat through the heavy surf. Four trips later, all aboard were landed safely on the beach.

A few days latter the steamer North America off loaded some of her cargo in an effort to lighten the vessel, so she could be pulled out into deeper water. Unfortunately, by this time the *Pascual's* hull was filled with water and could not be pulled off the bar.

This wreck is better known as the *Bone Wreck* and is also sometimes called the *Surf City Wreck*. She sits in 20 to 30 feet of water 200 yards off the beach in Ship Bottom. Much of her cargo which includes the many animal bones she was transporting can be seen scattered around the wreck. According to diver George Dreher, the law states that diving is only permitted when no lifeguards are on duty. Diving this site is best when done by boat.

RJUKAN

DIRECTIONS: **(Bradley Beach, Monmouth County)**
Take the Garden State Parkway to Exit 100. Take Rt 33 East. At the fork bear left onto Corlies Ave. Stay on Corlies to Main St and turn left. Turn right onto Newark Ave to the end. Turn left onto Ocean Ave. The wreck is located off Ocean Ave in front of the Bradley Bingo Hall.

CONDITIONS:
The 160 foot long, 960 ton Norwegian vessel *Rjukan* was en-route from London to New York, on December 26, 1876, when a strong northeast gale carried her into

Sketch of the *Rjukan* wreck site. Courtesy Howard Rothweiler.

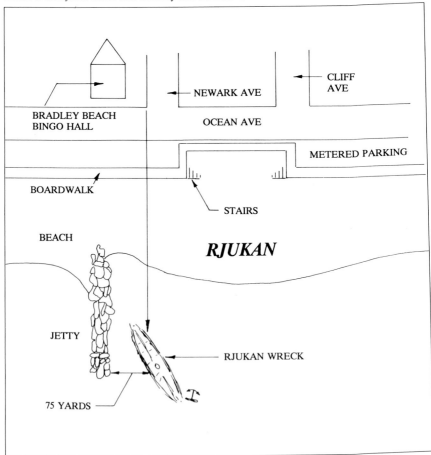

Rjukan wreck site. Photo by Daniel Berg.

Brass spike on the *Rjukan*. Photo by Kevin Brennan.

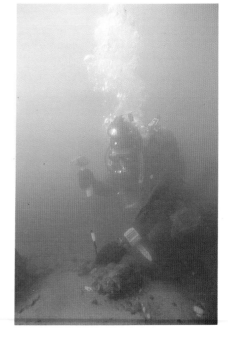

Dan Berg using a sledge hammer and chisel to recover artifacts. Photo by Jozef Koppelman.

the beach. At 6:30 AM, a beachcomber noticed the stranded vessel and called for assistance. Before help could arrive the violent seas caused her bow to turn leaving the ship broadside to the beach. The huge waves quickly destroyed her main, fore and mizzen mast and sent them crashing onto her deck. The lifesaving crew arrived at the scene but did not have a lifeboat. Fortunately for those aboard a local sea captain seeing the confusion launched his own vessel and by making several trips to the doomed *Rjukan* rescued all twenty crew members. By nightfall, the vessel had been broken apart by the heavy surf.

Today, the scattered wreckage of the *Rjukan* lies 200 feet off the beach in front of the Bradley Bingo Hall in 25 feet of water. According to Bill Davis, author of the book, SHIPWRECKS OF THE ATLANTIC "this wreck is one of the easier to locate and is a great dive for the novice and expert alike. The *Rjukan* is located off the jetty just south of Newark and Ocean avenues. Swim directly off the pavilion north of the jetty, keeping the northern wall of the pavilion in line with your offshore swim. Swim out parallel with the jetty until you reach the jettie's end. From there take a southeast compass heading, descend and swim in a southeast direction for approximately 50 yards. The wreck is large enough that it should be easily located." According to Howard Rothweiler, most of the wreck is very low to the sand. The wreckage is wood planking held together by brass spikes of various size and scattered around the wreck site there are ballast stones. There are two major sections of the wreck, both being approximately sixty feet in length and about thirty feet apart.

RUSLAND

DIRECTIONS: **(Long Branch, Monmouth County)**
Take the Garden State Parkway to Exit 105 East. Take Rt 36 to the end and turn right on Ocean Ave. Drive south for 2.5 miles, you will see a red church on the right. The Alfonso Retreat house is opposite the church. Note that parking may be a little tricky. I have parked in the dirt lot behind the retreat house on several occasions and have never had a problem. Please remember that this is not public property and divers should use manners, courtesy and good common sense when diving in the area.

CONDITIONS:
The Red Star Line steam ship *Rusland* was built in 1872, by Dundee ship builders in Scotland and originally named the *Kenilworth*. She was 345 feet long, had a 37 foot beam and displaced 2,538 tons. At 11:20 PM on March 17, 1877, under the command of Captain Jesse De Horsey, the Red Star steamer ran aground. A moderate gale was blowing from the northeast at the time, and a heavy sea prevailed. According to a statement from Captain De Horsey the *Rusland* had

The Red Star steam ship *Rusland* was built in 1872, by Dundee ship builders in Scotland. She was 345 feet long, had a 37 foot beam and displaced 2,538 tons. Photo courtesy Steamship Historical Society Collection, University of Baltimore Library.

This rare photograph was taken a year after the *Rusland* went aground. Photo courtesy Frank Litter.

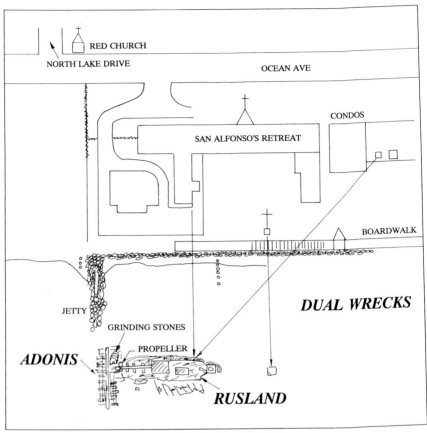

Sketch of the *Dual Wreck* area. By Howard Rothweiler and Daniel Berg.

sailed into a dense fog, "the weather was thick with an occasional snow squall." "At 9 o'clock 20 fathoms were found and sea cakes were brought up. As these cakes have never to my knowledge been found west of Fire Island, I concluded that the vessel was off the Long Island coast." "Twenty - five minutes later the lookout cried Light on the port bow! I thought that a mistake had been made by the sailor, as there should have been a light on our starboard bow." "I telegraphed for the vessel to be put about. Before this could be done, however, she struck." According to the NEW YORK TIMES, "The vessel headed straight on the beach, and keeled to the starboard side. She filled with water immediately afterward, and, from the volume which rushed in, it is supposed she must have struck a rock, making a hole in her hull."

She was carrying 200 passengers and a cargo of plate glass and iron wire from Antwerp to New York. Rockets were discharged, which attracted the attention of

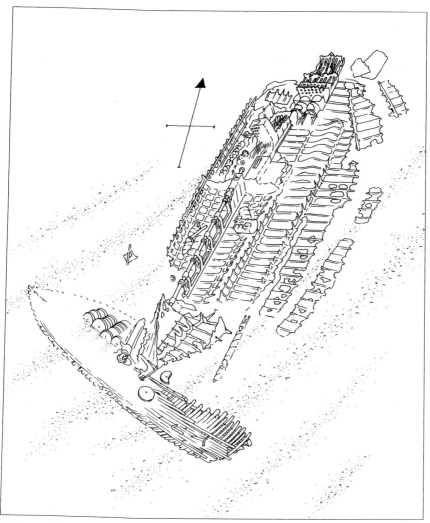

Underwater sketch of the *Adonis* and the *Rusland*. Courtesy Dan Lieb.

Lifesaving Stations No. 4 and 6. After many fruitless efforts, the lifesavors finally succeeded in getting a line over her bow. The apparatus for propelling a lifesaving car was quickly attached and the slow work of hauling passengers ashore started. By 10:00 AM, the next morning all the passengers and crew had been transported to the beach in the "lifesaving car." Only two people could be conveyed in the car at a time.

At first salvage crews anticipated no problem pulling the liner off the beach. It was later discovered that the ship was stuck fast onto the sunken wreck of the *Adonis* which had come ashore twenty years earlier. On April 8th, the *Rusland* finally

Rusland

Divers Dan Lieb (left) and Rick Schwarz at the site of the *Rusland* wreck. Photo by Daniel Berg.

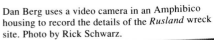

Dan Berg using a compass to navigate to the *Rusland*. Photo by Jozef Koppelman.

Dan Berg uses a video camera in an Amphibico housing to record the details of the *Rusland* wreck site. Photo by Rick Schwarz.

Rick Schwarz (left) and Dan Berg after diving the *Dual Wrecks*.
Photo by Dan Lieb.

Dead eyes, pump, wine bottles and porthole rim are
from the *Rusland*. The lead bar was found on the
Adonis wreck. Photos courtesy Frank Litter.

gave in to the constant pounding of the shore breakers and broke in two. This wreck along with the *Adonis*, are together known as the *Dual Wrecks*. They now sits in 25 feet of water just offshore and north of the tip of the jetty.

The *Rusland's* bow is facing north. At the south end of the wreck divers will find her steel propeller almost on top of the *Adonis* wreck. If you follow the propeller shaft north, you will be lead to her boiler. The boiler is the highest relief on the wreck and is easily recognizable. There is another boiler about 50 feet north of the first that sits in the sand away from the main wreckage.

SEASIDE PARK PIPELINE

Sketch by Howard Rothweiler.

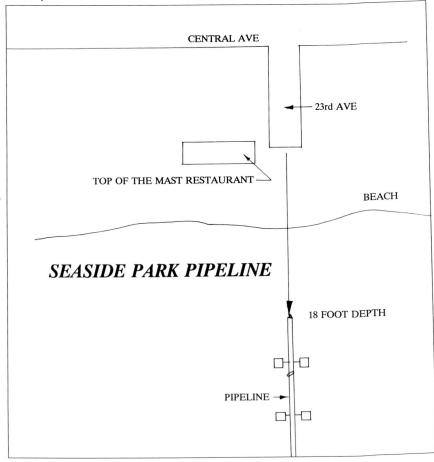

DIRECTIONS: **(Seaside Park, Ocean County)**
Take the Garden State Parkway to Exit 82. Get on Highway 37 East. Stay on 37 past the Tunney and Mathis Bridge. Turn right and head south on Central Ave. Turn left onto 23rd Ave to the end. The pipeline is directly offshore of 23rd Street.

CONDITIONS:
Located a few feet north of the Top of the Mast restaurant in Seaside Park, this old *Pipeline* now serves as its own fish haven. Howard Rothweiler and Bill Davis learned about this site from fellow diver, Joe Paolo. Howard and Bill visited the *Pipeline* and were happy to find an abundance of black fish, fluke and even a few lobsters. The black fish were surprisingly large and abundant for such a close to shore shallow site. Depth ranges from ten to over 25 feet.

As a side note there are many of these abandoned pipelines all along the Jersey coast. Each would be worthwhile to explore especially for spear fishing.

SHARK RIVER INLET

DIRECTIONS: **(Avon/Belmar, Monmouth County)**
Take the Garden State Parkway to Exit 100. Head east on Rt 33 and after crossing under Rt 18 bear right onto West Sylvania Ave. Take this to the end and turn right onto Main Street. Turn right on 5th Ave to the end and turn left on Ocean Ave.

CONDITIONS:
This is one of the most popular beach dives in the state. Diving is best at high slack when maximum depth is about 40 feet. Divers should begin their entry no earlier than an hour and a half before slack. This way the current should not be to powerful. This site is home to a full range of marine life and is popular not only for lobstering but also for underwater photography. According to diver, Bill Schmoldt, one of the best lobster hunting areas is on the outside of the " L " on the Avon side. Bill goes on to say that this inlet is one of the better New Jersey inlet dives because of less tidal flow. He also reports of seeing many tropical fish in the fall months. Howard Rothweiler agrees on the abundance of marine life on these jetties, since routinely spotted during their dives have been blowfish, sundial, summer fluke, winter flounder, ling, black fish, bluefish, stripped bass, squid and many other species to numerous to mention. In late summer and early fall various tropical fish make their way into the inlet. For those divers wishing to collect these tropical species for their aquarium, the most plentiful is probably the Atlantic banded butterfly. Divers will also commonly spot queen angle, soldier fish,

Shark River Inlet

Shark River Inlet is one of the most popular beach dives in the state. Photo by Daniel Berg.

Sketch of *Shark River Inlet* area. By Howard Rothweiler and Daniel Berg.

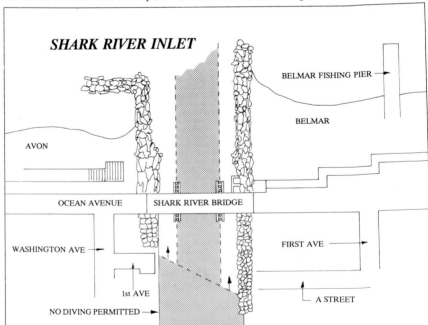

In the fall months divers can find a wide variety of marine life, including many tropical species. Photos by Jozef Koppelman.

squirrel fish and nassau grouper.

Divers should observe the following regulations when diving *Shark River Inlet.* First; divers must stay within 25 feet of the jetties and mark their positions with a dive flag. No diving is permitted in the inlet between 8:00 AM and 5:30 PM from May 1st through October 1st. Diving is only permitted in the area east of an imaginary line extending from the end of A Street in Belmar to the southeast end of First Ave in Avon (refer to diagram). Please be aware the regulations can change at any time so it is recommended to check with local municipalities before planning to dive here.

S.S. THURMOND

Sketch by Howard Rothweiler

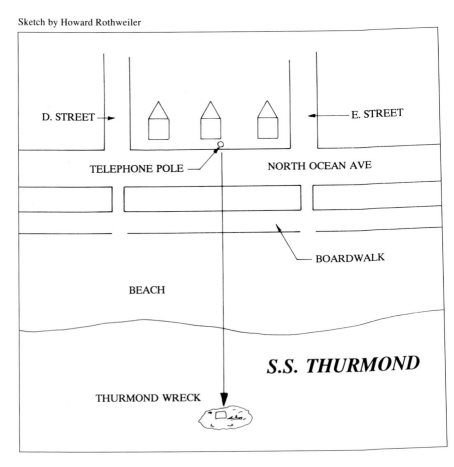

The *Thurmond* ran aground on December 25, 1909. Photo courtesy Bill Davis collection.

DIRECTIONS: (Seaside Park, Ocean County)

Take the Garden State Parkway to Exit 82 B, Rt 37 East. Stay on Rt 37 over the bridge then bear right at the fork. Turn left onto "N" Street to Ocean and turn left on Ocean. Take Ocean Drive to "D" Street. There is plenty of metered parking available. The wreck is between "D" and "E" Streets.

CONDITIONS:

The whale back steamer *S.S. Thurmond* was built by the American Steel Barge Co. in 1890. Originally named *Colgate Hoyt*, she was 276.5 feet long, had a 36.1 foot beam, displaced 1,253 gross tons, and was powered by a single screw compound steam engine. In 1907, the *Colgate Hoyt* was re-named *Bay City* and then in 1909, re-named for the last time, *Thurmond*.

On December 25, 1909, Christmas day, while en-route from Newport News, to Portland, Maine, and towing three schooner barges loaded with coal, a storm struck forcing the *Thurmond* to cut loose her tow. The *Thurmond* then turned to pick up the five crew assigned to each barge, but only rescued the first five before all three barges sunk, taking the remaining ten crew members to their watery graves. While searching for survivors in the blinding snowstorm, the *Thurmond* ran aground on the bar just off Seaside Park. According to Bill Davis's book, SHIPWRECKS OF THE ATLANTIC, "the next morning when beach master

71

Captain Henry Ware of Toms River made his morning rounds, he spotted the vessel and called his men to assist in the rescue." At first they thought that the vessel could be saved but before any attempt was made the *Thurmond* broke apart.

Today, the wreck lies in only 14 feet of water, 200 feet off "D" Street in Seaside Park. Divers will find her two large boilers to be the most significant and recognizable features on the site. For years this wreck was known as the *Boiler Wreck*. It wasn't until 1984, while Bill Davis, Ed Eglentowicz and Joe Paola, were researching wrecks sunk in the area when they uncovered what they believe to be the wreck's true name, *S.S. Thurmond*.

TOWNSEND INLET

DIRECTIONS: (Sea Isle/Avalon, Cape May County)
Take the Garden State Parkway to Exit 13, Rt 601. Take Rt 601, Avalon Blvd to Ocean Drive and turn left. Continue on Ocean to the bridge linking Sea Isle with Avalon. Park at the foot of bridge on the Avalon side.

CONDITIONS:
Dividing the south Jersey resort towns of Sea Isle City to the north and Avalon to the south is *Townsend Inlet*. The inlet is quite unusual compared to those of the north as it has two seperate jetties on the south side and none on the north.

The first jetty is located on the south side of the inlet at the foot of Ocean Drive bridge. At high tide, the inlet could be entered on the west side of the bridge from the beach, which makes for an easy beach entry. At high slack or low tide a diver could swim around the bridge pilings and retrieve mussels. The rocks of the jetty are not piled like *Shark River* or *Manasquan Inlets,* instead they are scattered. This makes for an excellent shelter for various fish that inhabit the area. Lobsters are also common here as they have made their homes amongst the rocks.

The second jetty is located one half mile east of the first and is a little more difficult to dive. The area is exposed to the ocean currents and surf. When conditions make it accessible, divers will be rewarded with good visibility. Black fish and sea bass are found in abundance with the occasional bluefish and stripped bass.

Diving both locations could be rewarding. As with all inlet dives the diver should be knowledgeable about tides and currents. Boat traffic is normally heavy during the summer months, therefore, diving should be done with caution. The maximum depth at this site is 25 feet with visibility averaging ten feet.

Photo courtesy Jozef Koppelman

UNDAUNTED

DIRECTIONS: **(Island Beach State Park, Ocean County)**
Take the Garden State Parkway to Exit 82 B, Rt 37 East. Stay on Rt 37 over the bridge then bear right at the fork. Continue into Island Beach State Park and Park in section A-12. Take the path over the dunes. The wreck is located 50 feet south of the path.

CONDITIONS:
On December 26, 1913, the 307 foot, schooner barge, *Undaunted* and another schooner barge, the *A.G. Ropes*, were being towed by the tug Edgar F. Luckenbach. A fierce Christmas gale was blowing and the captain of the tug decided to cut his tow free. He signaled to Captain Fickett of the *Undaunted* and Captain Olson of the *A.G. Ropes* to drop anchor and ride out the storm. Shortly after, both barges were washed into the breakers and pounded into pieces. Unfortunately, all ten crew members perished in the frigid waters. The *Undaunted* now lies scattered just outside the surf off Island Beach State Park.

The *Western World* ran aground in a heavy fog on October 22, 1853. Photo courtesy Bill Davis collection.

WESTERN WORLD

DIRECTIONS: (Spring Lake, Monmouth County)

Take the Garden State Parkway to Exit 98. Take Rt 34 South to the first traffic circle, then make a left onto Allaire Rd. Allaire will change into Ludlow Ave. Stay on Ludlow to the end and turn right on Ocean Ave. The wreck is located directly off the base of Jersey Ave. Parking is available on Ocean Ave.

CONDITIONS:

The British sailing ship, *Western World* ran aground in a heavy fog on October 22, 1853. At the time she was en-route from Liverpool to New York with 300 passengers. All of her passengers and crew were rescued. The steam tug, *Achilles* was dispatched to the scene and reported that the ship was lying with its bow to the north, broadside across the beach. Attempts to save the vessel were in vain.

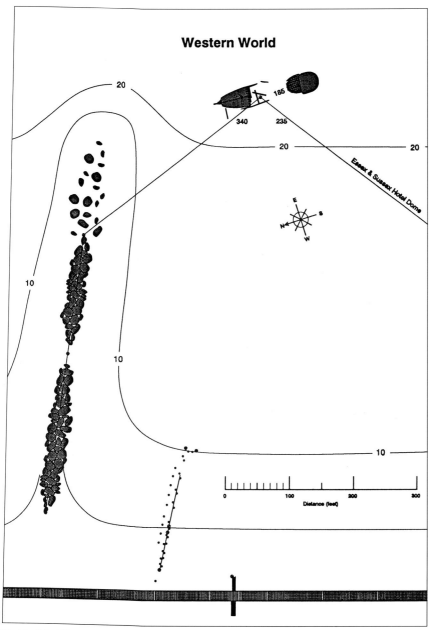

Sketch of the *Western World* wreck area. Sketch courtesy Mark Promislow.

On October 26th, the *Western World* broke apart and slipped beneath the waves. The wreck of the *Western World* is also known as the *Spring Lake Wreck.*

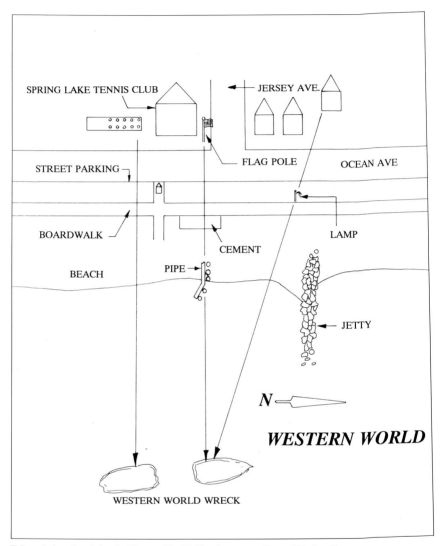

SPRING LAKE TENNIS CLUB

JERSEY AVE.

STREET PARKING

FLAG POLE

OCEAN AVE

BOARDWALK

LAMP

CEMENT

BEACH

PIPE

JETTY

N

WESTERN WORLD

WESTERN WORLD WRECK

Triangulation sketch for the *Western World*. Sketch courtesy Howard Rothweiler.

This wreck sits approximately 250 yards off the beach in 23 feet of water. She is covered with pieces of china embedded into a rock hard conglomerate. The first two divers to explore the *Western World* were Charlie Stratton and Howard Rowland back in the 1960's. These early divers found the wreck covered with china and artifacts. Her true identity was discovered around the same time that diver Ed Maliszewski recovered her bronze capstan cover back in 1962. After the capstan was recovered, divers researched the site and identified the wreck as the *Western World*. Back in the 1960's divers recovered everything from powder

Rick Schwarz (left) and Dan Lieb at the *Western World* wreck site. Photo by Daniel Berg.

Diver Howard Rothweiler on his way to dive the wreck of the *Western World*. Photo by Janet Lonza.

Western World

flasks, spurs, hinges, drawer handles, files, latches, china and silver trays from the site. Some china recovered from the wreck was manufactured by Felspar, in Burslem, England. Diver, Dan Lieb, reports that the wreck now consists of two congealed lumps.

In order to dive the *Western World* you must obtain written permission from the Spring Lake Chief of Police.

Dish recovered from the *Western World*. Photo courtesy Frank Litter.

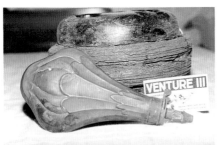

Spurs and buckels recovered from the *Western World* wreck by Paul Hepler. Photo by Howard Rothweiler.

Paul Hepler recovered this powder flask from the *Western World*. Photo by Howard Rothweiler.

Ed Maliszewski recovered this bronze capstan cover and converted it into a standing lamp. Photo by Daniel Berg.

Dishes and decorative brass curtain holders recovered from the *Western World* by Ed Maliszewski.

SUGGESTED READING

Other Books by the Authors

Berg, Daniel
  Wreck Valley
  Aqua Explorers, Inc. (1986)

Berg, Daniel
  Shore Diver
  Aqua Explorers, Inc. (1987)

Berg, Daniel and Denise
  Tropical Shipwrecks
  Aqua Explorers, Inc. (1989)

Berg, Daniel
  Wreck Valley Vol II
  Aqua Explorers, Inc. (1990)

Berg, Daniel and Denise
  Bermuda Shipwrecks
  Aqua Explorers, Inc. (1991)

Berg, Daniel
  Shipwreck Diving
  Aqua Explorers, Inc. (1991)

Berg, Daniel and Denise
  Florida Shipwrecks
  Aqua Explorers, Inc. (1991)

Berg, Daniel and Denise
  New Jersey Beach Diver
  Aqua Explorers, Inc. (1993)

Berg, Daniel
  Long Island Shore Diver, 2nd Edition
  Aqua Explorers, Inc. (1993)

SUGGESTED VIDEOS

Dan Berg's DIVE WRECK VALLEY Video Series

U.S.S. San Diego
Aqua Explorer Productions. (1991)

Rum Runner, Lizzie D.
Aqua Explorer Productions. (1991)

Kenosha, Lobster Dive
Aqua Explorer Productions. (1991)

Pinta
Aqua Explorer Productions. (1991)

R.C. Mohawk
Aqua Explorer Productions. (1992)

Bronx Queen
Aqua Explorer Productions. (1992)

Propeller Salvage
Aqua Explorer Productions. (1992)

U.S.S. Algol
Aqua Explorer Productions. (1992)

U.S.S. Tarpon, North Carolina
Aqua Explorer Productions. (1992)

Relief Light Ship
Aqua Explorer Productions. (1992)

H.M.S. Culloden
Aqua Explorer Productions. (1992)

Mistletoe
Aqua Explorer Productions. (1992)

INDEX